Divorce Laws For The Single Daddy

The Ultimate Guide To Divorce Law Basics To Get The Most Of The Divorce Process

Nick Thomas

JOIN OUR COMMUNITY!

Single Daddy Dating is a growing community of single fathers who look to help each other, not only with dating success but in all areas of their lives too. This includes parenting, career and finances advice.

Join us today and get '**10 Crucial Checklist To Dating Success For Single Fathers**' completely FREE!

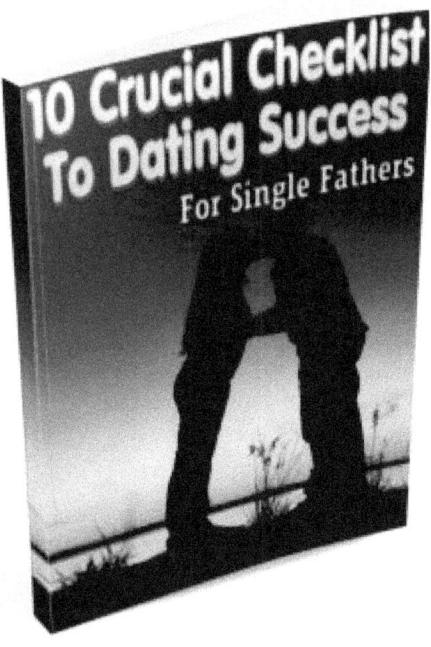

JOIN US AT
WWW.SINGLEDADDYDATING.COM/
NEWSLETTER/

CONTENTS

Chapter 1: What To Expect From A Divorce

As someone who has been a community of single fathers for many years, I have talked to many single fathers that has been very fulfilling.

They have shared with me their challenge with divorce, parenting and any other issues which bothers them. I feel happy to be able to help them and I know that even if I'm not a legal expert, being there to hear their problems make them feel better about their situation.

From experience, I can vouch that divorce

seems to be a one-sided decision which catches most men off-guard. Although I am lucky to be in a marriage that ended harmoniously, not many do. There were differences between my ex-wife and I, but we managed to get a common ground and work for the benefits of the children.

Rarely do married couples come together and decide to end a marriage together. In many situations, the husband would struggle with the consequences of a wife who is filing for divorce. He can't believe that after sharing so many wonderful years together, things simply end.

He would feel rejected, and this is a huge blow for him emotionally. He might have sleepless nights and worry endlessly about how this would impact the children.

There are also other concerns like not being able to protect his legal rights over his children, because the Family Court system seem to favor women during the divorce process.

The divorce process is a testing legal process that confuses many men. During this testing period, you would need to put aside your negative emotions, even if there seems to be an avalanche of unwanted emotions during the moment. One of the most important thing for a man when dealing with these divorce matters is to not let the emotional matters interfere with the legal issues.

If you have already gone through a divorce proceeding, you would have a better idea what to expect. If you haven't, the steps that you would need to go through during the divorce process would be dependent on the state you are in. Every state has different divorce laws and each country would also have its own procedure.

A great divorce lawyer would be able to explain and go through the entire divorce process to make it easier for you. First of all, you would also do some research beforehand. *Do you have a rough idea about how a divorce proceeding would be?*

One of the biggest mistakes that men facing a divorce make is to expect their divorce lawyers to explain everything to him. Although it is his/her job to do it, it is better if you know what to expect before you even find for a lawyer.

If you are the one filing for divorce instead of your ex-wife, you may be thinking that you need some 'grounds' for the divorce. For many states, this need has been done away with. This is more commonly known as a 'no-fault' divorce.

Every state has its own divorce laws which states the conditions that are grounds for divorce. There has got to be a clearer reason to end a marriage. For some situations, it can be as simple as 'irreconcilable difference'. This reason means that one party in the divorce is of the opinion that the marriage has broken down beyond saving. The other spouse's opinion doesn't matter.

In a 'no-faults divorce' it helps to keep emotions out of divorce court. This helps ensure divorce can be smoothly done through the Family Court System. I would discuss more about it in the future few chapters.

Besides these reasons, the following reasons are also commonly used in a grounds for divorce:-

- Sexual misconduct

- Adultery

- Alcoholism

- Drug Addiction

- Mental Illness

- Withholding Sex or Carnal

Abandonment

This book would give the man thinking of a divorce the basic knowledge about what to expect when thinking about a divorce. You would know what to expect and the steps to make before deciding to get a divorce.

Having this knowledge helps because it would save you time from having your expensive lawyer explain everything to you.

Over the years, I have seen many single fathers suffer from the effects of their mistakes made during the divorce proceeding.

That is why I decided to write this book to share with men looking for a divorce or already after a divorce. It would help them understand the divorce proceeding better and plan a better one.

This book is written with simplicity in mind. I wouldn't want to write a lengthy book that doesn't focus on the essential of a divorce proceeding. During such a tough situation, many men would find it cumbersome to read a heavy book about divorce.

It also has some other divorce considerations that you never expected. Read through to understand more about your situation and what to expect in the future.

Chapter 2: The Various Types Of Divorce

There are various kinds of divorce, depending on the situation you are in. You would need to consider what kind of divorce would suit your situation. Understanding the kind of divorce you are going for would allow you to focus more on the actions to take.

Ideally, your lawyer would be able to advise you better. He or she would listen to your situation and advice you on the best course of action. However, it still helps to know these different types so you have a rough idea what to expect.

Among the different types of divorce include:-

(1) No-Fault Divorce

This 'no-fault' divorce was created by the state of California in the 1970s. It makes it easier to get out of a marriage. Before that, the court need to find for a 'fault' in the marriage before a spouse could leave the marriage.

The 'fault' is simply the grounds for divorce. This include the few reasons mentioned in the previous chapter. There are still many states that still allow fault divorce and take into the wrongdoing of a spouse. Most also allow a no-fault divorce.

Simply put, no one is at fault for the marriage. The reason for this sort of divorce is simply incompatibility or having differences. There don't have to be any other explanation or proof that the marriage should continue.

(2)Uncontested Divorce

Uncontested Divorce happens when both the spouses decide to end the marriage on a mutual agreement. This means that the both of them are also able to come to an agreement about how to divide the property, children and other financial issues.

Such divorces are easy, simple and quick. However, it tends to favor the women better. Many men give up rights they didn't know they had during such divorce.

This include rights that may benefit the ex-wife too. This includes alimony, pension benefits and other sources of income. As such, a man should always consult a lawyer to play it safe.

(3)Limited Divorce

A limited divorce is similar to a legal

separation (which would be discussed in the next chapter). This isn't allowed in some states. This divorce simply give each other time to settle their issues.

Similar to a legal separation, the both spouses must live separately and can't have sexual relation with other people or each other. The benefits of this divorce is that it would give both of them time to come to an agreement on certain issues before the divorce becomes final.

(4) Simplified Divorce

A simplified divorce is a divorce where there isn't any contest and is a 'no-fault' divorce. This happens when there aren't any conflict between both spouses.

A simplified divorce normally happens when the marriage is for a short duration where there aren't any children and almost no assets to bicker over. This sort of divorce is cheaper and can be granted very quickly – usually within 30 days of filing.

***

These divorces are examples of divorces. However, there are many divorces which would be contested and go into court. Some of these can go on for years where both parties are relentless in the pursuit of what they want.

Chapter 3: Legal Separation & Divorce

A legal separation doesn't put an end to a marriage. Simply, it enables you to live separately while remaining married. It is possible to live separately while remaining legally married. During this 'separation period', both parties can discuss the issues such as division of assets, child support, child custody and alimony.

The very issues that are normally addressed in the divorce proceeding would also need to be addressed in a separation agreement. The purpose of a separation agreement is to protect your interest until a decision is made to file for divorce.

Besides that, this agreement would also set the precedence for the divorce that may follow. Similar to how my friend Adam puts it, a legal separation is to a divorce as an engagement is to a marriage.

Get a better idea now?

It is like a 'trial' before the actual divorce. If you get a divorce after a separation and the case goes into court, the judge would assume that you are satisfied with the separation agreement and it would carry over to the divorce settlement agreement. Because of this, you need to take time to consider the terms of the separation agreement as it would hold its weight in court.

Having a legal separation can have great

advantages rather than divorcing straight away. Among the various benefits includes:-

- **Allow Time Apart.** There are times where couples simply need some time apart to realise what they want. A marriage can become so tensed because they don't have a break from each other. A legal separation can give them time to realise how much they mean to each other, or otherwise. They help determine if a divorce is what they really want. If divorce is something suitable after the end of this period, only would they proceed with it.

- **Retain Other Benefits.** During a legal separation, benefits such as medical benefits or other benefits would still be maintained. Unlike a divorce which totally splits everything, a legal separation won't. Thus, this gives a better 'trial period' of divorce.

- **Social Security Benefits.** If you are

married for more than ten years, you can benefit better from certain social security benefits. These benefits normally are given to a 'married couple'. You would still be able to benefit from them while being separated compared to being divorce right away.

- **Religious Reasons.** For some religions, being divorce is a taboo. Having a legal separation allows you to maintain your marital status for religious purposes.

- **Conversion To A Divorce Settlement.** If both of you decide that a divorce is the best thing, the legal separation agreement can be easily converted to a divorce settlement agreement.

Legal separation is a good step if you want to 'test out' a divorce. Many fathers I know have said that they have saved their marriage by having a temporary break from the marriage. They realize how much their ex-wives mean to them.

For other single fathers, a legal separation also allows the transition to divorce easier. It allows both the single father and the wife to discuss potential issues. You would be able to have a better post-divorce life after the divorce settlement is done.

Chapter 4: Steps In A Contested Divorce

When both spouses aren't able to come to an agreement about the issues of a divorce, there would be a contested divorce. The issues that would need to be considered include division of assets and child custody.

During such situations, the litigation process would take way longer. If the spouses can't agree, a divorce mediator would be hired or the proceeding would go to court. The court would make the final decisions then.

For a single father, it helps to have a rough roadmap about the process of divorce. In this chapter, you would have a better idea about the steps in a contested divorce.

Step 1: Meet With Lawyer

It is important to find a lawyer that suits you. You need to find one that is qualified, trustworthy and whom you are comfortable with. You must be able to share your situation with him or her easily. You need one who isn't afraid of sharing his or her opinion.

During this process, the lawyer would gather all documents that would impact the divorce decision. This includes documents regarding the assets, children's documentations and other considerations. The lawyer would then determine what he or she feels is suitable for you.

Step 2: Divorce Petition

Then, the divorce petition would be prepared and file in court. Once this petition is filed with the court, the lawyer will then serve it to your spouse.

This can be served in person or by mail. If you can't locate your spouse, a notice will be published in local newspapers. After that, you will need to wait for some time before moving on to the legal process of divorce.

Step 3: Spouse's Response

Your spouse would need to respond to the divorce petition within 30 days, according to most state laws. If your spouse doesn't respond within that time frame, she would be deemed to be in default and you may obtain a default judgment. Should your spouse respond, the case would proceed to the next stages.

Step 4: Discovery Stage

This stage is when the spouses would be able to gain more detailed information about each other. This includes income, custody, assets and other issues pertaining to the divorce situation.

This is done through written interrogations, deposition and document requests. During this period, a concern that parents would have is to have temporary orders for alimony or child support.

Step 5: Settlement Stage

Ideally, the judges would try to encourage the spouses to agree before the final court date. A third party would try to mediate between two parties to negotiate any unresolved issues. If a settlement is unable to be made, the discovery stage would continue and the case would be brought to divorce court.

Step 6: Divorce Trial

During the divorce trial, each party would be able to examine each other side's claim. This include putting on witnesses and make closing arguments. The state laws and the amount of divorce cases pending in the local Family Court would determine how quickly the case goes to trial.

During the proceedings, the judge would listen to both parties and come to a suitable conclusion regarding all issues. The length of time the judge takes to come to a final order would be determined by how complex your case is.

Step 7: Post-Trial Motions

Once the trial is over and the judge has filed the divorce order, either party can file a post-trial motion for relief from the final judgment. You would have 30 days after the order is signed to file this motion while the other party would have another 30 days to respond.

Step 8: Appeal

If post-trial motions are denied, an appeal can filed within 30 days of the final judgment or 30 days after the denial of post-trial motions.

The party that is seeking the appeal would have a few months to file the lower court record with the appeal courts and file his/her brief. A month would be given to the other party to file a response brief.

In many states, the parties would be granted an oral argument and then the court would make the final decision. If the case is reversed, the appellate court would send the case back to trial court for further proceedings.

However, if the case is affirmed, it is considered over. The divorce decree would be final.

Chapter 5: Understanding Your Legal Rights

Like I have said before in many chapters, it is important for you to check your state divorce laws as your legal rights would differ between the different states. Although your rights are protected by the Bill Of Rights and other divorce proceedings rights in the country, you need to put in some effort to have more knowledge about your situation.

We all have the common right to not be abused, intimidated or harassed. To avoid these situations, laws are set in place to prevent such behavior.

You also need to avoid doing certain things out of your negative emotions. No one should ever do the following during the divorce, regardless of how difficult the divorce is:-

- **Don't Harm Or Harass Your Spouse.** Should your spouse become violent, you can apply for a restraining order. Having a restraining order would make it easier for you to call law enforcement officers. If you feel like you are in a violent position, you need to get help immediately. You need to protect yourself. There is this myth that men are the only ones who tend to get violent in a marriage. This isn't true. Women can be very violent too.

- **Don't Damage Or Transfer Assets Owned.** If both of you own certain properties or other valuable assets, it is important to take care of it. You can't dispose, destroy or conceal it to protect your own interest. If the judge finds out, you would leave a bad impression on the judge.

- **Don't Move Your Minor Children.** Don't move your children outside the jurisdiction of the court. This can give the impression that you are trying to abduct them. This would create a bad impression in the eyes of the judge.

- **Don't Hide Minor Children From Your Spouse.** During the divorce period, your spouse would still have rights to meet your minor children unless specifically stated. Make your children available to visit and don't make it hard for them.

- **Don't Disregard Temporary Court Orders.** During the divorce period, temporary court orders are important if your spouse has a history of violence. It would help alleviate any anxiety and protect your legal rights. If your spouse try to cross any boundaries, this temporary court order would prevent her.

These are all ethical conduct that you should follow during the divorce proceeding. It is not only that you should protect yourself from things that your spouse would do to you, you also need to avoid doing them as well.

Doing such things would put yourself in a disadvantaged position as far as divorce proceedings go.

Chapter 6: Divorce Strategies

When dealing with a divorce, there are two main strategies that people and their divorce lawyers employ. According to Herb Guggenheim writing for Capital M, there seems to be two main strategies that would be shared in this chapter.

Reciprocal Altruism

This divorce approach is based on the idea that when you do kind things for other people, they will do kind things back for you.

This is similar to the Golden Rule which is 'do unto others which you would have them do unto you.'

This approach means that you treat the divorce in a kind manner, and your ex-wife would do the same. She would see your kindness and think that's things have only gone bad which are completely out of your control. When both parties use this approach, the divorce can be settled easily.

Such an approach would help your child get over the divorce faster too. They would see that both their parents are being civil to each other and that they are working together for the child's benefits. Deep down, the child would know that he/she is still loved by both parents.

What's In It For Me

This approach means that you see the world

as a hostile place, a dog-eat-dog world where only the strong survive. This means that you would do everything that you need to get what you want. It doesn't matter if you need to step all over other people (in this case, your ex-wife).

When using this approach, there is a tendency that things get tensed. If both parties decide to use this approach, the divorce would get very tense. Both parties would try to do whatever possible to deal with the other person and get what they want.

Many contested divorces come from this mindset. Both spouses want to win because they felt like they have been hurt from the other party. When you approach the divorce in such a manner, do you know suffers the most from it? The children.

Your children would be stuck in the middle and would have trouble trying to cope with the emotional rollercoaster of the divorce.

They feel that the family becomes a very hostile environment.

***

Which approach would you choose then?

Being kind matters, because you want to be able to give the best for your children. You want to deal with the situation kindly so you can more over from the divorce and live a different life.

But, you don't want your ex-wife to step all over you too. There are some situations where the ex-wife would treat you like a fool and try to do whatever possible. They would be selfish and try to get whatever they want. They would cross every boundary possible because they simply don't respect other people.

What approach which is suitable then?

A mixture of both. Be kind, but also have

boundaries when dealing with the divorce. State clearly what you do and do not accept. Be firm about it, but be polite.

Chapter 7: Financial Advice For Men Facing A Divorce

A man needs to protect himself during a divorce. There are some ex-wives who are so emotionally charged that she would try her best to get EVERYTHING from him.

I have known single fathers who lose everything during a divorce proceeding because they lack the foresight to see what could possibly happen in the future.

These are few financial matters that would matter to you, if you are facing a divorce:-

1. **Bank Accounts.** If you have a joint bank account with your spouse, go to the bank and divide it in half. Deposit half of it in your own name. If you put everything in your name, it would leave a bad impression on the judge if he or she finds out. As a single father, you want to have your children's needs taken care of. You would need to leave your spouse with some money.

2. **Stocks.** For stocks, mutual funds and bonds that are jointly held with your spouse, you would need to call your broker and divide the stock. You would also need to divide future taxes too.

3. **Inventory.** List out everything you have in the house with a video tape or take pictures. Date the inventory and include everything as detailed as possible. This is

to ensure your ex-wife wouldn't take something away in the future. If she takes it, you would have evidence for it.

4. **Valuables.** If you have any valuables such as painting, jewellery or heirlooms; move them to another place. Make sure that your ex-wife don't have easy access to these assets, especially those that have significant or sentimental. Your intention isn't to hide things. Rather this is to ensure that things won't get lost during the divorce proceeding.

5. **Documents.** Your documents are important. Move them to somewhere else like to a friends' house or lawyer office. Doing this is important because your ex-wife might look for evidence to blame you for the divorce. She may also steal some documents and blame you for it.

6. **Safe Deposit Box.** Use a safe deposit box if you can't find a trustworthy friend to

save your documents. If you already have a safe deposit box which is jointly held with your ex-wife, get another. You wouldn't want her to have access to it.

7. **Credit Cards.** There are times where the spouse would have a supplementary credit card (from your credit card). You wouldn't want to wake up one day to know that she has spent $20,000 on the card and you would need to pay for it. Cancel the card as soon as you can. Tell your spouse about this and tell her she can use the money in the joint bank account to pay for expenses.

8. **Insurance.** If your insurance policy cover your spouse or children, don't drop them from the policy until the divorce is final. You would want to be responsible for their medical bills too. In many situations, single fathers would still want to be responsible for this even after the divorce is finalised. If you are in charge of child support, any unexpected medical expense

would be charged to you. That is why it is important to have your children adequately covered for medical insurance.

9. **Pensions.** Retirement funds acquired during the marriage is considered a marital asset. This would need to be divided in divorce court. Both of you would share the retirement fund. As such, you would want to request your employer to stop contributing this year as you wouldn't want your ex-wife to get anything after divorce. You would need to set up a different retirement fund post-divorce. This fund would be completely yours.

10. **Get A Lawyer.** You would need to search for a divorce lawyer that is qualified and trustworthy. This is an important step even if it costs you a lot of money. This would saves you from headache in the future. The lawyer would advise you that he or she would need to review any documents before you sign it.

Many of these tips may make sense to you, but you have never thought about it. This is common when you have so many things on your mind. Do them, if you feel they are applicable. It would save you a lot of heartache in the future.

Chapter 8: Pro Se Divorce: Is It For You

A Pro Se Divorce happens when you represent yourself in a divorce litigation, without the need of an lawyer. The procedures are the same for a regular divorce, only difference being that you would be responsible on your own when it comes to filing the legal forms.

This divorce method isn't popular because most people have no idea what to do. However, there are still some situations where a Pro Se Divorce can be applicable:-

- When a man totally can't afford a lawyer.

- When a man has an uncontested divorce, without any children or assets.

These are the two common reasons when a Pro Se Divorce happens. Another uncommon reason why this happens is when some people become dissatisfied with the lawyer in the past. They have had such a terrible experience with lawyers that they completely don't want to get a lawyer.

If you truly decide to proceed with a Pro Se Divorce, you need to consider the legal and emotional aspects of a divorce first. If you can't keep it separated, you must hire a lawyer.

Too many times, men become too emotional with their divorce that they simply can handle their emotions to think logically. They wouldn't be able to represent themselves in court then.

A divorce would impact their finances, children and self-esteem in the future. If not handled properly, issues such as division of assets, child custody and alimony can have dire consequences.

No one would admit that divorce proceedings are easy. Even experienced lawyers get a headache sometimes from all the paperwork. Therefore, if you truly decide to use this method, make sure you are ready. Only choose this method if you are really sure about what to expect.

If you choose this method, you would need to know in depth the specific law in your state legislation, Rules Of Civil procedure, the Family Court Codes in your state and the other rules following your local country court. To get this information, the best place would be the state law library or approved websites.

Yes. It can be that complicated. That is why it is best to hire a divorce lawyer if you can hire one. This book wouldn't go into details about how the Pro Se Divorce is done, but I would just like to make sure that this is an option for any men considering a divorce.

But before you decide to follow this route, make sure you aren't in any of these situations. If you are, then getting a lawyer would be better. These situations include:-

- **Did your spouse hire a high-priced lawyer in court?** Should your spouse hire a high priced lawyer, this is an indication that she is really taking the divorce proceeding seriously. A good lawyer can easily make you pay. The courts won't care who is right or wrong. A good lawyer can easily make you the 'bad person' in the marriage and make you pay heavily for it.

- **Are there huge assets involved?** If there are many assets involved, you would definitely want to hire a lawyer. When multiple assets are involved, there is a tendency for complication in terms of valuing the property and division of assets. Such matters are complicated and it is better to leave it to someone experienced.

- **Do you have many children?** If you have many children, you need to consider the various effects. Child custody can be very tricky. There would be plenty of considerations that you never thought of in the first place. A lawyer would be able to ask you about it and see where you stand in various situations. Going the Pro Se route can be dangerous because you may lose custody of all your children.

- **Has there been any violence at home?** If there has been domestic abuse or suspicion of child abuse, you should know that these issues would make divorce more complicated. You would want to settle these issues well to ensure it won't impact your children in the future.

- **Do you live in a different state from your spouse?** Things can be different if your spouse files for divorce in a different state. If she files for a divorce in another state, the state laws applies. You need to have a lawyer who is familiar with those laws to ensure the process is smooth.

- **Are there issues of addiction or mental illness?** Again, these issues can make things complicated. If she has a history of drug addiction or mental illness, she may act irrationally. You need a competent lawyer who protects your rights as well as your safety.

Pro Se Divorce is a risky path that can be filled with landmines and potholes. Rarely do I see a divorce situation where a Pro Se would be feasible.

Even if you have a 'one night marriage', like celebrities, you should not go the Pro Se route. You may save money now, but it would cost you in the future.

Chapter 9: Collaborative Divorce

A collaborative divorce is an option for married couples who wish to negotiate their divorce, instead of litigate. Collaborative divorce is a new form of alternative dispute resolution that has become popular recently.

It allows couples to have control over their divorce while working with several 'experts' that would help them explain various situations. They would then collaborate to make sure the needs of everyone are being met.

Using this approach involves finding a **Collaborative Divorce team** that helps the couple identify divorce goals, objectives, obstacles and solutions.

In such an approach, the main focus is on the needs of the entire family and to make sure they transition well. The real focus is on the well-being of all family members, especially the children.

In my experience, there are some divorces where this approach can help. Some mature people simply realize that their marriage failed simply because things have changed. People change, and they don't want such a thing to impact their other family members.

In such a situation, a mediator would be very important as he or she would play an important role in getting both parties to talk civilly. Whenever there are difference in opinions on issues such as asset division, child custody or alimony; their roles become important to resolve any disputes.

For such an arrangement, you and your spouse would negotiate an acceptable agreement with professional help. Each of you would hire a specially-trained collaborative lawyers.

The lawyers would advise and assist both of you in negotiating an acceptable settlement. You would meet separately with your lawyer and she would meet with yours. After that, the four of you would meet together regularly to reach an agreement. This process may also involve other professionals such as accountants or child custody specialist.

In most cases, should there be no settlement reached, the lawyers would not represent you if it ends up in divorce court. You would need to find another lawyer who would take your case to court.

If an agreement has been met, you would still need to meet a family court judge. He or she would sign the agreement to finalize the divorce.

Through the process of collaboration, you would keep the contact brief. The legal process would be simple and uncontested. A trial or litigation hearing won't be needed.

In short, a collaborative divorce has multiple benefits if it suits your situation. You would be able to:-

- Stabilise the divorce when both of you decide to file for divorce. This is done through a temporary agreement.

- Voluntarily exchange the required information, so as to not waste anyone's time.

- Cut down on legal expense by agreeing on the legal procedures.

- Negotiate a fair settlement which serves the both of you.

- Being able to talk things through, instead of using a lawyer for communication which can be very expensive.

A collaborative divorce is something that is recommended if you and your spouse are in good talking terms and that both of you are on the same page. Both of you should realize that the marriage ends without any resentment. From such a divorce, you get to save a ton of money and time.

LEAVE A REVIEW

I hope this book has helped you well. It isn't my intention at all to go deep into the topic. I am no expert in everything. However, I have the help of many other single fathers who have shared with me their invaluable experience.

If this book has helped you in any way, do leave me a review. This helps build our single father community.

If you feel that this book can be improved in any way, do mention it in the review. I would love to hear from you.

I wish you luck as a single father…

ABOUT NICK THOMAS

Nicholas Thomas has helped many single fathers cope with divorce in the past few years. By helping them gain more confidence and stability in their lives, he is able to guide them towards being a man that attracts other women easily.

He divorced back in 2008 and knows how difficult a divorce can be for a man. It was a terrible time for him when he got his divorce. He envisioned his children blaming him and not being able to spend time with him. It gave him a constant guilt trip.

Being a divorced man can be very difficult. Ever since his 'emotional recovery' from the divorce, he has helped many single fathers by advising and helping them gain confidence.

Should you want to share your story with him, you can do so at
www.singledaddydating.com/shareastory/

ALSO BY NICK THOMAS

(1) Dating After Divorce For The Single Daddy

(2) Dating Ideas For The Single Daddy

(3) How To Be An Alpha Male

(4) First Date Conversations

(5) Online Dating

(6) How To Approach Women

(7) Mature Dating

(8) Single Parent Support

(9) Coping With Divorce

(10) Parenting After Divorce

Visit www.singledaddydating.com/bookstore/

Get Your Complimentary
FREE BOOK

Join our community today and get **10 Crucial Checklist To Dating Success For Single Fathers** FREE, delivered right to your email…

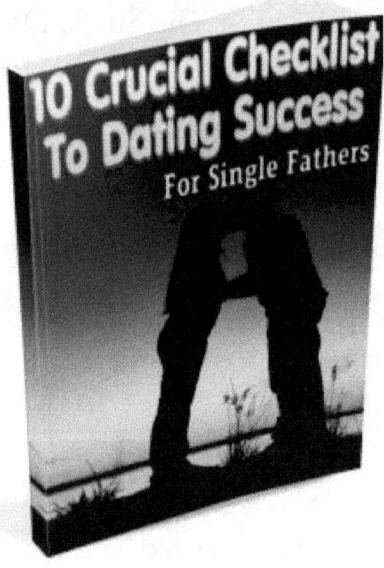

JOIN US AT
WWW.SINGLEDADDYDATING.COM/ NEWSLETTER/